I WISH YOU WOULD!
LETTING GO OF MY PAIN

Sandra K. Bridges

Copyright © 2025 by Sandra K. Bridges

All rights reserved. No part of this book may be reproduced or used in any manner without written permission of the copyright owner except for the use of quotations in a book review.

First paperback edition June 2025

ISBN 979-8-218-76758-7 (paperback)

Published by Sandra K. Bridges

Dedication

I would like to dedicate this book to my mother, Mrs. Jerlene Magee Bridges. She was a phenomenal woman, wife, mother, sister, daughter, and friend. She worked in her community and her Church (Ephesus Seventh Day Adventist Church). She loved to cook and bake cakes and pies for her family and whoever stopped by the house. She worked for years at Ochsner Medical Center, where she was well loved.

Mom also gardened and had her children helping her in the garden. She even went to night school to learn to sew clothing for her six children. Mom made all my baby brothers' baby clothes. My mom even sewed my sister's and my outfits for church and special occasions. When my sister and I were preparing to go to college, she sewed outfits for us. We were the best dressed freshman on campus! Our mother showed her love in so many ways to all she met. I hear her speaking to me at times when I'm cooking. If I'm going through a rough patch, I remember something she said or did.

I understand that God is guiding me and inspiring me. This book is dedicated to those women who know that they have the power to change their circumstances. These women will not allow fear to keep them down. They will rise like a phoenix!

Mom passed away from breast cancer that spread to her brain in October 1983.

Please remember to get your mammogram every year and do your self-exams at home!

Acknowledgments

This project would not have been possible without the inspiration of the Holy Spirit!

I'm grateful for the gift that has been given to me. I would like to thank Uncle Bernard Bridges and others for encouraging me to write this book years ago! Although it took longer, it's worth the wait.

Thank you to my big sister Gwen Bridges for sharing my poetry with others. Thank you to Aunt Audrey Wiley and all my friends for their encouragement throughout the years! To all my writer and author friends, thank you for your positive reviews of my book. They were very helpful to me. To my family and friends, know that I love you and that I appreciate your advice over the years. It means a lot to me.

Peace & Blessings

Sandra Kay Bridges
Skay4real

Table of Contents

Table of Contents	5
Preface	1
Section 1: Becoming Me	3
The Power of a Good Woman	4
I Am Who I Say I Am	6
Go into Your Closet	8
Giving the Best of Me	11
I Am Happy Being Me	13
Filled with Pride: A Black Woman	16
Reflection	18
Section 2: Meditation	20
Take Me to the King	21
Staying on Course	24
Joy Is Powerful	26
Holding on in Faith	29
What Would You Do?	31
Standing in the Light	33
Reflection	34
Section 3: Worth It	36
Do You Feel Me?	37

Woman to Woman	39
Enough	42
All I'm Asking	45
Beautifully Made	47
Reflection	49
Section 4: Devotion	**51**
He Came to Visit	52
Letter of Recommendation	56
Speaking Sound Doctrine	58
In the Morning	60
Understanding My Faith	61
Hope Beyond the Grave	62
Give Thanks	63
Look to the Hills	65
A Mother's Prayer	67
Climbing Your Mountain	70
He Blessed Me Still	71
I Praise His Holy Name	73
Prayer Changes Things	75
Reflection	77
Section 5: She Said That	**79**
I Wish You Would	80
The Devil in Disguise	82

Is It You or Is It Me?	84
I Want That Ride and Die Type of Love!	86
Go If You Want to Go!	89
Fed Up	91
Don't Try Me	93
Hold This Tongue Of Mine Lord! Hold It for Me!	94
Reflection	96
About the Author	98

Sandra K. Bridges

Preface

Throughout history, women have been underestimated, misunderstood, and often misrepresented. Yet, time and again, they have risen, defying expectations, shattering barriers, and standing their ground with grace, faith, and unshakable resolve. This book, *I Wish You Would!*, is a testament to the enduring power of women—a tribute to their strength, resilience, and unyielding spirit.

At the heart of this strength is a faith rooted in the power of Jesus Christ. With His guidance and the powerful prayers of women standing together, no obstacle is insurmountable. It is this divine connection that has empowered generations of women to rise above adversity. They have leaned on their faith, calling on the strength of Christ and the support of each other to persevere, overcome, and thrive.

From the pioneers of the past to the trailblazers of today, women have continuously shown that they are not to be underestimated. They are leaders, warriors, nurturers, and innovators, navigating life's challenges with both courage and a deep spiritual foundation. The prayers of strong women, lifted to Christ, have the power to move mountains, heal hearts, and inspire transformation.

This book brings together the voices, stories, and experiences of women who have dared to say, "I Wish You Would!" Their strength does not come from defiance alone but from the confidence and faith that God is with them. In every trial and triumph, they rise—supported by each other and by the unwavering love of Jesus Christ.

As you read through these pages, may you find inspiration in the diversity of women's experiences and the common thread of faith and resilience that binds us all. This is not just a collection of stories—it is a declaration of the divine power within every woman who believes, prays, and rises in the name of Jehovah Jesus Christ, our Lord!

Section 1: Becoming Me

I Wish You Would!

The Power of a Good Woman

A good woman knows her worth.
She does not have to be told that she's a good woman.
She's a power broker, a mediator for a large corporation.
She multitasks, a CEO and a CFO. She runs Wall Street!
A good woman knows her worth.
She's always immaculately dressed.
She's coiffed and her nails are polished.
Her makeup is flawless, and her skin is soft and without blemish.
This diva is powerful and wanted by all corporations.
She can run countries all by herself.
A good woman knows her worth.
When she is confident and dressed to impress, she can get any man's attention.
She's built to withstand all the storms that life thinks to bring her way.
She can nurse her babies and then take care of her man late into the early morning hours.
This chick is bad!
A good woman must have a good man by her side.
She does not tolerate a weak-kneed man.
She will not even glance his way.
It takes a powerful, self-confident man to take care of a good woman.
She will allow him to be the head of her household.

She will allow him to take care of her and the family.
She will stand confidently by his side at all times.
Please don't mess with her man.
A good woman loves strong and long.
So if you desire to be with her, you must come correct with your application completed and all prerequisites achieved, because a good woman is hard to keep!

I Wish You Would!

I Am Who I Say I Am

I am who I say I am.
I more than just I am.
I am that mountain that you want to climb,
I am that valley that you walked through,
I am the thoughts of yesterday,
And the prayers of tomorrow.
I gave birth to a nation.
I am who I say I am.
I am determination and wisdom,
I am your sons and daughters,
I am your hopes and your desires,
I am all of your needs and your wants,
I am all that you hope to be.
I am who I say I am.
All you need or want to be!
I am a conquering hero,
I am a fighter and a mighty warrior,
I am the realization of your dreams come true,
I am a person of sustenance.
I am powerful and knowledgeable.
I lead men where they don't want to go!
I am a power that a man cannot control!
I can and have brought down many nations.
I am a teacher who taught a man to be a man!
I am who I say I am.

I never need to be identified or pacified by anyone.
Others cannot find the terms or phrases to
describe me, for I am indescribable!
I am everything a weak man does not want me to be!
A ruler of nations and of worlds!
If you don't know me by now, you never will!
I am who I say I am.
I am strong, I am powerful,
I am determined, I am intelligent,
I am independent, I am a lover,
I am a teacher, I am a nurturer.
I am everything you think I am,
A man's weakness and his strength.
I am his hopes and his desires.
I am his Amazon in and out of bed!
Never doubt who rules this world,
Never doubt that I will always be here.
Who am I?
I am who I say I am!
At last, I am Wo-man.

Go into Your Closet

"But thou, when thou prayest, enter into thy closet, and when thou hast shut thy door, pray to thy Father which is in secret; and thy Father which seeth in secret shall reward thee openly" (Matthew 6:6 KJV).

Have you ever been told to go in your closet and get rid of all your baggage or old clothing? What does that statement mean to you? Think about it. I was told this by a, shall we say, "friend"! We were having a "discussion" about relationships between a man and a woman. What does a man want in a relationship, and what does a woman want in a relationship? He stated he wants commitment and partnership. His woman was going to hustle like he does and put her money in the budget with his. His woman would have to take care of the kids and the house and HIM!

Now, that did not sit well with me. I believe in sharing and sharing alike. If I do it, so can the man! I stated I've been there and done that, and I must have a true partner willing to give their all to me and the relationship. I stated, "Trust is a valuable commodity to me. I will not accept lies and deceit from no one and nobody. I refuse to live with a drunk and an abuser. No one will smoke anything in my home around me and my children." Well, this statement did not go over well with him! He said I called him a liar and compared him to my other men. He stated I needed to go into my closet and throw out all of my baggage and call him when I was done. He got up and left me sitting and wondering what the hell he was talking about. So, the next day, I called him and asked him to explain his statement.

When we have been hurt by someone that we thought loved us and cared about us, that is a blow to our egos and our hearts. It's confusing and disappointing to think that someone you committed your life to would deliberately hurt and take their love from you! You grieve and go through the process of a dying relationship. It's like putting that part of your life in a grave. It hurts like hell! So, you must go through the process of letting go of that part of your life. Letting go of the anger, pain, disappointment, dreams, plans, pain, frustration, and heartache. This process will take time and much prayer. Yes, you will cry many tears, and fear might enter into the process. Trust is another factor in letting someone else into your personal space. It takes time to heal from the death of a relationship, and it will take time to forgive the other person. But you must forgive them for your sake, not theirs. You cannot hold on to that anger and pain. It can and will make you sick or kill you. If you hold on to that pain and anger, the other person is still controlling your actions!

Yes, they are because you are letting them dictate whether you will start to live your life or if you will keep them with you by holding on to your hurt pride and anger for them. Let go and let God heal you! Let go and let God send the right person to you. Clean out and throw away all that excess baggage of anger, hurt, pride, and confusion. Go out and find a new hobby and meet others. There's no harm in being scared to start over. It feels like going on your first date in high school. It's conquering your fear of starting something new and fresh. It's exciting and frightening all at the same time. Who knows what can happen or what you will discover about yourself. Live in the moment and begin to trust you again. Time does heal all wounds and egos. Go into your closet of hurt and pain, place them in a garbage bag of forgiveness! Then place them on the curb so that the garbage truck can pick them up. You will feel so much better. When you see that other person in divorce court or on the street, just smile and say hello! Keep walking with your head held high with that big smile on your beautiful face. I did that and it felt wonderful!

Sandra K. Bridges

Giving the Best of Me

Every day, I give the best of me.
I dedicate my entire life to you.
I toil the earth to provide for you.
I give you the best of me!
Without a plea or cry, I gave all of me.
I make decisions based on your needs.
I always consider your wants and desires.
I gave my all to you, my body and my soul!
I never think of me because it's about you.
I live to please you and only you.
I desire to give you the best of me.
Tell me what more I can give to you.
How much more can I please you?
My love and devotion, I give freely to you.
What can I do to make you love me?
Why won't you give your love to me?
I ask you for the last time, why do you hurt me so?
I prayed and asked God to direct me.
I begged Him to forgive me.
I placed another before Him!
I am so confused and stressed.
I am weary and afraid, by the life choices I have made.
I know my Father cares for me.
I trust and I do love him!
God told me, "I love you. You are my child!

I made you perfect in every way.
I accept you because I designed you.
I love you just because!"
So, my dear, since I cannot please you, then I must leave you.
After all, I only want the best for you.
I now give me the best of myself.
I now know and understand,
I must take care of the very best.
That's my God and me.
For He saw only the best in me!

Sandra K. Bridges

I Am Happy Being Me

I am happy being me because I love me the best. I have learned to accept who I am and what I am, and that's the best! It's about accepting my inner and outer self and loving them both. I am unique and beautifully made by the original designer. I am like no other! When I smile, you don't see anything fake. You see someone who is truly happy with themselves. In loving me, I can love you more! When I am content and satisfied with my life, I can spread my joy to the world. The sun shines brighter. The stars twinkle like diamonds in the night sky with the happiness that I feel just being me.

It feels good to be me. My soul is content, and I am at peace with me. My mind is no longer confused, and now I can think clearer. Now I see what my Father was attempting to show me. He was pointing out how wonderfully made and magnificent I am. I could not see my true self because of my unwillingness to accept who I was. It is marvelous to be me; my soul is sanctified and satisfied with who I am. I have discovered my peace in the depths of the valley floor. I have climbed over the mountain of depression and discovered my peace of mind!

I no longer accept anyone's deceitfulness and deception of so-called love. I no longer crave to be accepted into everyone's circles. I no longer desire to be manipulated and handled by the insignificance or the minuteness of another! I am worth more than that! I denounce the stupidity and the inability of others to rationalize who I am at this point in my existence! I have no need to explain my choices in hopes that they will compromise their rules and regulations so that that I will fit into the boxes that they have constructed. Why should I? I'm just being me!

Beautifully made and beautifully magnificent to behold!

If my Heavenly Father did not compromise His beliefs and His Peace just to fit into the temples and synagogues, why should I compromise my choices and beliefs? I do not have to be part of every click, club, and group! We all are uniquely made and shaped by the Master's hands. I have owned that, and now I live that! I have come this far by faith and His Grace. He has allowed me to see who I am and whose I am! I was blind, but now I see His grace and His mercy! What a remarkable feeling, to feel my savior's grace.

My love and my life. All He wants for me is everlasting peace. All He wants to give me is His Father's Love. All that I now desire is to give myself solely unto Him. I am nothing without Him, and I am everything with Him. I am humbled by Him! He has become my all, and my life is everlasting. He is the only man that has kept His promises to me. I love this man!

So, I will not abandon Him, and I will not be who society wants me to be. I will not change who I am to fit man's criteria of who they think I should be. I will never whimper and cry in the night because man cannot or will not accept me. But, I will pray that one day, you will allow my Father to visit you soon. My prayer is that one day you can discover what I discovered, tranquility, peace, and understanding! Most of all, I pray that someday you will discover His Love for you.

I am happy being me!

Filled with Pride: A Black Woman

A Black Woman is the best thing to happen to a man of any color, tribe, race, or creed.

She is a formidable warrior, mother, and a dedicated employee.

She is purposeful, task-oriented, and an entrepreneur.

She is a woman of many hues, builds, and talents.

Her eyes are like no other.

Her hair comes in many textures, lengths, and colors.

Her skin has no wrinkles and is as soft as her baby's bottom.

A Black Woman is a nurturer by nature.

She is a caregiver by trade; she can cook a meal with less than five ingredients.

She has made miracles happen on a daily basis.

A Black Woman does not take no as the final answer.

She is stubborn.

And she is determined to have her say and her way.

You will change your mind when dealing with A Black Woman.

Warning: do not mess with A Black Woman's money, man, or child.

You will regret your error in misjudging A Black Woman.

She is a fighter like no other that you will ever see.

I repeat: do not mess with her home, child, and lastly, her man!

Her home is immaculate.

When she is at peace, she is filled with pride for herself, her home, and her family.

A Black Woman is the best person to have on your side in any situation because she will pray for your, sing you a song of praise for her God, and get you all the inside information on anything that is happening in the neighborhood.

She will beat you down and love you up when you need it. Just don't cross her too many times.

You just might be found in somebody's back alleyway.

A Black Woman can show up and show out at any time of the day or night.

You must be ready for her at all times!

Now, a Black mother is a whole nother thing, and you do not want her in your pathway.

When you see her, please run the other way.

If she finds out you did something to her child, I suggest you say your prayers.

A Black momma doesn't play like that.

You will have a group of Black mommas looking for you.

A Black Woman is the most beautiful, statuesque woman in the world!

She is the original model that all women are made from and trying to look like!

She is in all men's dreams.

A beautiful and dedicated sister is what they are searching for and some will dream of til eternity.

A beautiful Black Woman filled with pride.

Reflection:

Sandra K. Bridges

Section 2: Meditation

Sandra K. Bridges

Take Me to the King

"And in my prosperity I said, I shall never be moved. LORD, by thy favour thou hast made my mountain to stand strong: thou didst hide thy face, and I was troubled. I cried to thee, O LORD; and unto the LORD I made supplication. What profit is there in my blood, when I go down to the pit? Shall the dust praise thee? shall it declare thy truth? Hear, O LORD, and have mercy upon me: LORD, be thou my helper. Thou hast turned for me my mourning into dancing: thou hast put off my sackcloth, and girded me with gladness; To the end that my glory may sing praise to thee, and not be silent. O LORD my God, I will give thanks unto thee for ever" (Psalms 30:6-12 KJV).

I have been praying and telling God how much I am grateful for His favor and His blessings. And He has been so good to me and my family. If I had ten years to tell you how good He has been to me and my family, it would not be enough time! God is so good and so merciful to us stubborn and ungrateful people. For we do forget that He has performed miracles just for us! Not just once or twice, but continuously for our good! I reflect on how He has brought me through storms time and time again! I never want to forget from whence I have come. I never want to get so comfortable now that I forget to appreciate the whence. I want to tell others of "how I got over" and how I found peace within!

Here is how I "got over" my storm clouds:
1. Forgive yourself. No, I am not perfect.

2. Ask God for forgiveness.
3. Forgive those who YOU feel hurt you, betrayed you, lied to you. Forgive them. Release the hurt.
4. Let go of the past and look at the present. Pray for your future.
5. Let go of your weaknesses, e.g., shopping, men, women, food, whatever; let them go.
6. Repair your mind, body, spirit, and house (home); they need healing.
7. Rebuild your faith and trust in yourself and your God.
8. PRAY while you're cleaning out your closets that are holding old sins and hurts.
9. PRAY when you take those garbage bags of anger and frustration to the curbside.
10. PRAY; never stop praying and talking to the Father. Allow Him to comfort you while you are healing.
11. Find a place to be still, to listen for that still, small voice; a place of peace just for you and Jesus.

Yes, it took a lot of work and looking within at my faults and shortcomings. Yes, there was a lot to work on! Anger, bitterness, disappointment, mistrust, hurt, pain, and shame. But God! He is a forgiving God! I love myself so much better! I want to go to Heaven and be with my Father. That is my soul desire! We must dig deep so that we can remove that mess that is festering inside of us. We have to let go of what feels good and get what is good for our soul salvation. We must become strong and release the weak and scared person inside of us. We are queens and kings of the Most High God, and we deserve all that He has for us!

We deserve the best of the best! Question: How can you claim to stand firm for Christ and be a wimp and afraid to confront that which is keeping you held down in the pigpens? Jesus promised us that He would walk beside us wherever we are. He also said that He would be our protector and provider. Do you believe Him, or do you want to rely on yourself (man) to be your provider and protector? "Take Me to the King," sings Tamala Mann, Take me to the King so that I may kneel at His throne of grace!

I Wish You Would!

Staying on Course

We are taught to look left and to look right when crossing a street. We are taught to be weary of strangers in our neighborhoods.

We are taught to write our names and learn the alphabet. We are taught to count our numbers and learn our primary colors.

In church, we are taught to sing about the Lamb.

We are taught to say a few Bible verses and to perform the Christmas carols and the

Easter pageants. No one taught us how to stay on course in the battlefield of life. We needed this lesson!

Staying on Course is hard to do! Trusting and believing in Jesus is so easy for some of us. Yet, it is frightening for others.

It is so hard to allow your entire life to be drawn out and guided by another. It is powerful and humbling to bow down and fall prostrate in front of God.

Staying on Course will become easier when you just give God ALL your problems! You now understand that you are nothing without God, your Father.

You now understand that prayer and communing with Jesus daily is a necessity and not a want.

You desire to serve Him and not yourself.

Staying on Course is trusting and loving God more than you do yourself.

Staying on Course is an awesome experience because you are with Him continuously.

Staying on Course is an uplifting and joyous experience with Jesus.

Keep your eyes on the prize of salvation by Staying on Course with Jesus.

Joy Is Powerful

Today, I am choosing to be Joyful despite any storms that may arise. I am choosing to shout with Joy for my Lord. I am choosing to put all the negativity and sadness out of my mouth and out of my heart. I choose to be grateful, faithful, and filled with Joy! Why, you ask? Because my Father in heaven is my Joy. He is trustworthy, and He never, ever failed me yet!

I will not allow Satan and his imps to discourage me from being happy and take away my peace. I will not allow anyone or anything to stop me from experiencing my Joy and happiness! I defy and stomp on the devil's attempt to keep me down. I choose to dance with Joy, and I know without a shadow of any doubt that I am an overcomer! I have been in the valley, lying on its floor, filled with pain and sorrow. I have been in the pits of despair and depression. My Lord and Savior rescued me and brought me out of all that pain, sorrow, and despair. He filled me with happiness and peace and healed my sin-sick soul! I am grateful and Joyful for the love my God has shown me!

I have no reason to be sad or unhappy. I have no reason to be scared and frightened by the troubles that cross my pathway. For I know that my God can do all things. He proved that by being nailed to the cross for me. I must continue to show Him my love and faith, and I must trust Him! It is totally up to me to choose who I will serve and depend upon. It's either God or Satan that I will serve. I choose God to be on my team and to be the team leader!

This is why I keep a smile on my face. I don't trouble myself anymore with insignificant issues. I must focus on my walk with God and keep myself on the right track. If I can pull up my brother and sister along the way, then I will. But I will not allow anyone or anything to keep me off my pathway and my walk with the Lord.

Keep negativity away from you. Walk away quickly and do not entertain Satan's imps and foot soldiers. Keep the name of Jesus on your lips and in your heart at all times.

If you do this, then you keep away negative thoughts. Because good and evil cannot occupy the same space. Sing a song of cheer, sing a song of Joy and peace to keep negative thoughts out of your space. Satan cannot come into your space unless you invite him in. Continue to speak, for this and every season is a season of Thanksgiving!

I love each and every one of you, and I give thanks for the Lord bringing you into my space! My God has been good to me this day, and every day, He continues to bless me and heal my broken spirit and body! I shout Hallelujah for my victories and the testimonies I have gained thus far on my journey! I thank God for my pastor and his continued prayers and support. What a mighty God we serve! Keep up the good fight, and keep Joy at the forefront of all that you do and all that you say! Rain washes away our dirt and helps joy bring love into our souls so that the sun shines brightly in our hearts!

Joy came to me this morning. Joy now resides in peace!

I Wish You Would!

Sandra K. Bridges

Holding on in Faith

It is so hard sometimes to maintain and not complain of all my battles then, to encounter destiny from others.
Lord Jesus, please help me to hold on!
Oh, how do I continue to ask why?
Why can't I go here and there because I don't have money to pay for this and that?
The doubts and faults people throw in my face of why my God does not love me!
My God, my God! Who do these people think You are?
Don't they realize who they are cursing?
Don't they understand that You gave them life?
Jesus, where are You? I need You right now!
I need Your comfort and Your strength to sustain me in my fight to survive this hateful and hurt-filled life.
As I prepare to get away from these angry and vengeful creatures, I now hear Your voice telling me how much You love and cherish me!
I thank You once again for all Your devotion and care in my most vulnerable moments of despair.
I cannot wait to dance through Your pearly gates and to gain my crown.
My Father, I have no doubts that You care. I feel Your breath of life everywhere; I see Your love shining down on me.
Through the rays of the sun in the sky.
I hear Your words of comfort from the birds that sit outside

my window.
Your joy is in the bountiful colors of the flowers and leaves on the trees.
Your smile is in all the animals of the forest and the seas.
My Lord, I am holding on to my faith.
Though it's difficult in the face of my adversaries.
I will stand strong.
I am determined to continue this battle because of my faith and my love for thee.
You continue to bless me and my family.
You continue to encompass me in Your favor and heal my sin-sick soul.
I will always speak of Your goodness and Your mercy.
I will continue to testify of Your Holiness and unwavering love for us.
In spite of my weakness and doubts, You continue to bless me still.
I will continue to Hold on in Faith.
Steadfast is my trust and love for You.
You are my Savior and my redeemer!
I am Holding on in Faith.

What Would You Do?

What would you do if someone lied about you and it affected your good community standing? What would you do if someone falsely accused you of having an affair with their spouse? What would you do if someone accused you of homosexuality? What would you do if someone you know stole your money from your bank account? What would you do if these individuals told you, "But I love you"?

If it was me, I would be hurt, angry, confused, disillusioned, used, and mad as hell! I never said anything about turning to Jesus for answers and assistance. WOW! Jesus has gone through all these things. He was falsely accused so many times, and yet He quietly kept His composure and answered every one of His accusers and shamed them.

We forget about what our Heavenly Father went through and is still going through because of our lack of faith and trust in Him. He is waiting on us to come to Him for forgiveness, healing, and redemption. When we suffer, He suffers, and when we hurt, He hurts for us. He would love to hold us and dry our tears; but we must first go to Him for healing and serenity. He knows everything that is going to happen, has happened, and will happen on this vast globe. There is nothing that He does not know. He is called Alpha and Omega for a reason; He is called Creator for a reason, my brothers and sisters. Why do we forget that?

Why do we whimper and cry over things and want to hide

in a corner when trouble finds us? Why do we feel like pulling the sheets over our heads when trouble looms out on the horizon? Why? Because we lack faith in ourselves and in our GOD! Yes, we do that because we are human and have not given it all over to God yet. We are babies still in the nursery, and we have a long way to go to become more steady on our feet. But as long as we do not give up and we keep stumbling down the pathway toward Jesus, we are going to be fine. Just keep holding on, keep a prayer on your lips and a song in your heart! You will be alright.

Never forget whose child you are. Never give up on

yourself! Keep it moving. Keep it moving toward the cross! It is going to be alright! We must continue to persevere and support each other when we fall. We must pick up our brother and sister and love them back into the fold of Jesus Christ and keep on walking toward salvation in Jesus. Our God is a good God, a forgiving God, and a loving God. Remember, you are not perfect yourself, so please do not be so hard on your brother or sister when they fail you. I am not asking you to be a fool and turn a blind eye to negativity. Forgive them despite their shortcomings. It's for you and not them.

Sandra K. Bridges

Standing in the Light

(PSALMS 27)

I stand firm in the light of the Holy One! His light shines
bright in the morn and in the darkness of the night.
His light is the light that comforts and heals our minds, bodies,
and spirits.
Nature drinks His light and flourishes to feed all the
inhabitants of the earth. Goodness and mercy comes forth
through the light!
The light gives birth to all things! The light is our Heavenly
Father! Our Prince of Peace!
Standing in the light is amazing! I know that the light is our
blessed hope! I stand in His light of love, peace and joy!

Reflection:

Section 3: Worth It

Sandra K. Bridges

Do You Feel Me?

When I lay on the other side of the bed crying,
When I look at you and you know I don't believe your lies,
When you leave the house without leaving any money,
When you call to say you are working overtime,
When you think I am still your fool!
When you say you still love my smile and my hair,
When you walk out the room to answer your cell phone,
When you say you are going fishing with the boys,
When you say, "Not tonight, I'm tired,"
When you no longer look at me in that special way
When you think that I still believe all your lies!
When I say no to you now that you are in the mood,
When I say, I refuse to shed a tear over you,
When I tell you to go fix your own food,
When I tell you, I no longer need anything from you,
When I tell you I love me more than I love you,
Do you feel me?

I Wish You Would!

You never knew how to be a friend or my lover.
You did not understand that in order to keep me,
You had to feed me with love and devotion.
You had to give me attention and appreciation.
You had to pray with me and for our relationship.
You had to show me that I was your only woman.
You neglected me, and now our home is just a house.
Do you feel me? What? Did you find another?
I decided to not wait on you any longer!
Do you feel me?
I took care of me, and thank you for setting me free from no love and you!
I love me more, and thank you for showing me how to take care of me first!
Do you feel me? I do.

Woman to Woman

Sometimes, it takes another woman to tell a woman that it's time for a change in her life. It takes another woman to tell a woman, "I care about you. I am concerned about what you are going through." It takes another woman to tell a woman, "Stop and look at what is happening to you! Stop and step aside and allow me to help you!" Today is my day to say, "God, I need you! I need help to tell this woman to stand still and look at herself!"

Woman to Woman, you don't look too good today. Girlfriend, what's really going on with you? The stress of trying to keep all your mess together is really getting to you. Is it worth the hassle to try to keep a piece of a man? You must remember that there are two people in a relationship and not one. You don't have a relationship with only one person trying! Is it worth your health to try and please this so-called man? Who you know does not give a damn? Have you thought about how your children see you with this so-called man? Is this the image that you want your kids to view you? Woman to Woman, he's just not into you!

Woman to Woman, your girl-child is disrespecting you. She see's how that piece of man is treating and misusing you. You are worth more than gold. Yet, you are selling yourself for less than a copper penny. You are beautiful and magnificently made, yet you are allowing yourself to be treated like a slave! Woman to Woman, please stop allowing yourself to be used and abused. This man says he doesn't love you! Woman to Woman, you are God's holy child. So, why are you allowing Satan to live with your child?

Woman to Woman, you are precious and sweet as honey. Yet, you allow your home to become so bitter and unbecoming. You no longer have a home but just a house. Woman to Woman, please allow our Father to clean out your house so that your children can have a home. You deserve better than you allow yourself to have. You are a heavenly wonder and made to be loved and cherished by the man God has set aside for you. You are intelligent, educated, dedicated, and deserve to be loved and treated with respect and dignity. You are a queen and regal in stature, your Father is the king of the universe, and you deserve to be treated as royalty. You are a teacher and a healer. You are a giver and a comforter to many. Woman to Woman, love yourself enough to say, I have had enough. It's time for a change. It's time to clean my house out. It's time that I allow my Father to move Satan out of my house! It's time that I stop settling for less than the best. It's time I start taking care of myself and getting some rest."

Woman to Woman, I must love myself. Woman to Woman, I must be loved by the best.

Woman to Woman, I never loved him. He was just my mistake! Woman to Woman, I saw him hitting on you; yet, I did not say anything! It will never happen again!

Woman to Woman, thanks for being my friend.

Enough

I am tired and just cannot take it anymore.
I have done everything in my power to please
and understand your demands. I am weary
of the pain and humiliation you bring to me.
I don't know how much more I can take of
your hate that you bring into my house.
This is no longer a home of comfort
but a home of pain. It's a shame that I have
to whisper and watch what I say because
I am afraid of how you will react to
the fact that I have to pay all the bills because you won't.
I lowered my standards and lowered my
expectations of a man to try and explain why I am
still with you. I cannot and will not take this
treatment from you ever again! Please, stop
treating me this way! Why do you continue to

do this? You keep apologizing and say you will
do better by me. But then you turn back around
and hit me. If you do this again, I will leave.
Enough is enough, and now I am leaving you.
I just came back to tell you goodbye.
I have filed for divorce and left the papers
on the kitchen table.
No, I did not prepare food and drink for you.
Please do not raise your hand or your voice at me
again. You see, I can and will defend myself
if you try to beat me again. I just came to tell you
goodbye and I only want to see you in divorce
court. You can now be miserable all by yourself.
I have had enough of your lies and promises to do
better. You never loved me or respected me. I finally
understand that you were never my man or man
enough for me. You could never please me in or out
of bed. You don't know how to please a good
woman like me. So, goodbye and good luck with
the rest of your miserable life.
Enough is when you are sick and tired of being sick
and tired. Enough is when you realize you could be happy all
by yourself. Enough is when you desire peace within! Enough
is when you cry out to the Lord for deliverance from your pain
and sadness. Enough is when I looked across the breakfast
table at a man I literally hate to see chewing food I prepared
for someone who was supposed to love me!
Enough is when I allowed God to show me the way out of all
my hurt and pain. He showed me the path to peace and

understanding. He showed me joy and happiness. He showed me love unconditionally!

He showed me Enough.

Sandra K. Bridges

All I'm Asking

I have been true to myself and to you
Kept my word and stood by your side
Supported your work and all that you do
All I'm asking is that you support me too
Held you through all the tough times
Prayed for you, laughed with you
Read God's Word with you and trusted you
All I'm asking is that you hold me too
It's so hard to continue to give you my all
This relationship has become one-sided
My eyes have opened, and I see clearly now
You're unable to share yourself with me
All I'm asking of you is to show me you
I am giving you fair warning, my love
You will look for me and I will be gone
I will not and cannot continue to be used
I am not and will never be your fool
Please do not be confused by this attitude
All I'm asking is to be desired and recognized
All I wanted was to be your prize
Is it you, or is it me who is unwilling?
Am unable to say, "I love you" or "goodbye"
I will do the honors; "I love you and goodbye"
To someone who is not able to face who he is
A taker and someone who cannot love and trust

I Wish You Would!

All I ever wanted from you was love and trust
All I'm asking of you is
Say goodbye
So goodbye to love that was lost

Sandra K. Bridges

Beautifully Made

I was designed to walk the earth
and become the mother of all.
I was designed to be the queen
and rule the world. I am beauty itself, and
others try to model themselves after me.
They are envious of my stature
and my walk. You see, I am beautifully
made by the master.
I wear a coat of many colors and hues.
I have a curve in my back that no
others can duplicate. My lips and eyes come in
many shapes and forms. Men love the smooth
round fullness of my lips.
My breasts do impress the masses.
All try to duplicate them but never
achieve the shape and size of mine.
My thighs, well, they speak for themselves.
They are are like thick pieces of chocolate
that all men desire to taste.
My hips sway with the waves of the ocean.
All watch me walk and move as I
glide to my throne with grace. My hair comes
in many textures and lengths. Some try and
buy the imitation of my hair texture,
but it does not feel or look quite right.

I Wish You Would!

I am the queen of all, and I demand respect.
You see, I am an African queen who knows
who she is and is proud of what she is.
I am beautifully made and designed by the best.
I love me and I am proud to be me!
Beautifully made and lovely to behold.

Sandra K. Bridges

Reflection:

I Wish You Would!

Section 4: Devotion

He Came to Visit

I am going to visit a church today to see how many Christian friends I can meet! They say this church I will visit today is not a big church, but it's a church with potential, and it meets my needs.

I am looking my very best, and I am dressed to impress! I am wearing the latest and greatest in suits, socks, and ties! My shoes are shiny and polished, and my jewelry is sparkling with diamonds and pearls. I am ready to be seen and see who I can see.

This is a magnificent building, filled to the brim with beautiful people. Wow, the choir is out of this world, and the musicians are fantastic! The doorkeepers are really working and doing a great job! The church announcements are too long and drawn out though.

The elders are OK, and the prayer was long and dry! Let's get to the good part, the sermon! I want to hear what this preacher man is going to say. What is going on? This is not the pastor of this church. What did he say?

The head deacon is making an announcement: he said the pastor was not preaching today because the pastor is home ill. The pastor wanted me to remind the church to be weary of who you are sitting next to. He said, "God told him that Satan might visit the church today and to be watchful and prayerful of whose hands you shake on today."

The head deacon said, "If any of you are sitting next to a

well-dressed, smooth-talking, good-smelling man or woman, tell that person to get thee behind me, Satan! You are not welcome in my house or my Father's house anymore!"

Well, this caused a stir in the church because this was every woman, man, and child in the church! The church turned back to the deacon to ask how they can tell the difference between Satan and the church member?

The deacon said, "Take off your armor of clothing and give it to the poorest member of the church who does not have clothes such as yours." Well, they turned to the only family in the church they knew to not dress like them, and instead of taking off their best of the best, they gave the family money.

The deacon said, "That is not what the pastor asked of you. He said to give them your clothing." One woman said, "I am not giving that family my Dolce & Gabbana outfit that I paid $3000 for!" Well, several members felt the same way and walked out of the church, refusing to give up their expensive clothing.

Satan was jumping up and down in the church, laughing and clapping because he had won knew members for his church. Well, one of the members of the poor family walked up to him and said, "Satan, get out of my church and never return." Satan was shocked the member recognized him. He said, "How did you recognize me?"

The member said, "Because I see you a lot in my line of work. I am a grave digger and a stone carver. You are always walking around surveying the lay of the land. That's why I did not shake your hand or greet you at the door today. That's why I don't wear my finest to church. I do not want to be mistaken for someone like you! God wants me to be a unique and wonderful human being to everyone rich or poor and big or small. I do my best to serve everyone and help anyone that I can. I want to go home to heaven and not visit you in hell! Now, get out of my church and do not return here again!"

It's not what you wear or how much it costs, it's about how you wear what you have on the inside of you! The people who refused to give up their expensive clothing were shallow and materialistic. They wanted to be seen and feel important. It was about a fashion show! Christ was nowhere in them!

Now, the poor family was not really poor! They were rich in spirit, and they knew it was not about what they wore on the outside, but what they wore on the inside. They had Christ in them, and it showed on the outside to others! They knew what spirituality and salvation was all about. It's about shedding our outerwear and putting on our God-wears!

It's about Christ Jesus being inside us, shining so bright, it shines out of us in our speech, the way we walk and the way we talk. It's in our soul! Through Christ's sacrifice, we are invited into an eternal relationship with God.

I Wish You Would!

Letter of Recommendation

I am writing this
Letter of Recommendation
for Jesus Christ and His Team,
who are always on time.
He has never been delayed in His deliveries,
He has invaluable, dependable qualities,
His team work ethic is without question.
His character is flawless, His team shows up on time.
He always has a smile for others. His presence is calming and quiet. You feel His presence when you walk into any room.
I am instantly calmed because of who He is.
He knows when I am not feeling well.
He knows when I need a hug.
His team knows when you need protection.
Therefore, I recommend Jesus Christ to you.
He brings with Him a team that is like no other.
His team members are the Holy Spirit, who is
the team's motivational speaker and
company trainer. Then there is the Father;
the Father is the chief and president of the team,
Jesus is the front man and the problem solver.
This is the ultimate team for any organization!
This team is the best of the best.
They can drive up profit 1000% or more!
Jesus completes His tasks on time,

His profit and production is of the highest.
He would be a great asset to any company,
firm, or organization! He is the man you want
to use for recruitment! I highly recommend
Him and His team to your company! You will never
regret choosing this team over any other team!
I recommend that you take Him as
your Lord and Savior! You will testify to their
goodness and to their mercy.
You will testify to their grace, for it is like no other.
I highly recommend my Jesus to you!

Speaking Sound Doctrine

Be careful who you listen to! Their words and advice sound good, but do they really have your best interest at heart? One of my friends was going through some rough times medically. I told her that this individual said they were praying for her. A simple statement from a caring person. Well, my friend stated, "I do not want everybody praying for me, cause I don't know their intent or if their prayers will be sincere!"

I asked her what she meant by that. She explained, "Everybody who calls themselves a Christian ain't really a Christian. So, I don't know their intent or purpose. I can and will pray for myself." I just looked at her! Does she have a valid point? I really do not know.

I visited another church with my family. It was not the same religion as I was. But I'm of the opinion, if you follow, thus saith the Lord, we will be alright! Well, we were alright until the pastor started talking about Jesus Christ and the state of the dead. Ashes to ashes and dust to dust thus we will return. Our souls return to heaven. But we sleep the sleep of the dead. We don't come back and have conversations with our love ones or go to Heaven. God made us from dust and dust we will return until the second coming of Jesus Christ!

The Bible says the dead "know not any thing" (Ecclesiastes 9:5 KJV); they "do not praise the Lord" (Psalm 115:17 NKJV).

Be careful who you listen to! Know God's Word for your own well-being. No one can take that away from you.

There is a song, "smiling faces, they smile in your face and stab you in the back! Smiling faces all tell lies"…there is also a verse that says, "be careful who you entertain, for they might be angels in disguise"…

I suggest we all just keep a prayer in our hearts and on our lips at all times!

Have a blessed day, and may you always walk in His Spirit.

I Wish You Would!

In the Morning

In the wee hours of the morning
you lie awake, trying to figure
out what it will take to
ask God to forgive your mistakes.
You lay in your bed, crying and feeling
sorry for all you have done to
someone whom you love more than
yourself. You begin to talk and pray
to your Heavenly Father, begging and
pleading, "Lord, please forgive me."
Then a calmness and quiet comes over you.
You begin to rock back and forth.
Now you are at peace, and you slowly calm
down. You realize that the sun has risen
high in the sky. You hear the song the birds
are singing and begin to get ready
for the new day. A fresh start is what you
need. To show God that you have learned your
lesson. To always follow his laws and precepts.
In the morning light, God gives us a chance
to redeem ourselves and to begin again.
A fresh start to a better life!
In the Morning is a new beginning to a
better life in Christ!

Sandra K. Bridges

Understanding My Faith

Stand firm on the truth of God's Word. Trust Him, no matter what others may say. Real faith is standing firm and going to sleep in the midst of the storm. So stand firm!

My interpretation of faith is this:

I am walking blind on a street called Promise.

Following the directions a man I have never met gave to me. He told me He would never hurt, misuse, lie, or steal from me. Yet, He would give me everything that I need to live and survive in this world. He said people know Him by many names. He told me never to give up on His son, who is called Hope, and His assistant, who is called Trust. He stated that they would always be with me, even though I might not see them face to face. Yet, I will see their signs in nature and also high in the sky. He stated that He would send people to help me from time to time. But they will always be with me, even though I may experience rough times. I now have a real-lationship with this person called God. I now step out on faith and walk with the Hope of the cross by my side. I have placed all my trust in this man's son from Galilee.

Hope Beyond the Grave

The apostle Paul, in his famous chapter about the resurrection (1 Corinthians 15), stresses that the hope of the resurrection is an essential component of our total faith experience (vs. 12-19). If there is no resurrection, our faith is empty. We are left with lots of questions as we contemplate the life that awaits us. Questions that will never be fully answered here and now.

Yet we can learn from Jesus Christ's resurrection. It's important to note that the Christ who was raised from the dead was the same person as the one who, a few days earlier, died on the cross. He arose with a "glorified" body that was no longer subject to the laws of nature in the way our mortal bodies are.

And yet, we can also experience some of that eternal life now. Paul explains to us in (Romans 8:10) that the Spirit will enter the person who has turned to Christ. The believer, therefore, is already touched by the eternal life that will become a full reality in the world to come. The presence of the Spirit is the pledge of our eternal salvation (Ephesians 1:13-14).

Put your faith and hope in a perfect being who goes by the name of Alpha and Omega, HE IS the Lord of Lords, King of All Kings, Your ALL and ALL. He is a Mother to the motherless and a Father to the fatherless, a Teacher of all subjects, a Doctor who specializes in all treatments and procedures. He is dependable all of the time. He is trustworthy and always on time!

He is my Best Friend!

Try Him.

Sandra K. Bridges

Give Thanks

9 It is better to trust in the LORD than to put confidence in princes.
10 All nations compassed me about: but in the name of the LORD will I destroy them.
(Psalms 118:9-10 KJV)

No matter how many plans we put in place and how many times we check our to-do list, something always happens to delay or change our plans. This happened to me recently. I made plans, went through the correct channels, and prepared for my event. But God had a different path for me to follow. Everything on my list was canceled! I sat down and just called out to my Father (rather loudly). He spoke to me and told me to follow Him. He had a different road map for me to follow. I placed all my trust and faith in Him. All went well, and I accomplished my task with excellent results. I listened to that voice and prayed while going to my destination. I kept in touch with Him at every stop I made and every person I spoke to. I was comforted when the voice spoke to me and told me who to speak with to get the information I needed. I am telling you that we must stand still and pause for Jesus to speak to our spirit! It worked for me, and He prepared a way for me!

I felt at peace in His presence, knowing He was keeping me safe from harm! He went before me and placed others in my path to protect and guide me! What a gift to receive from the

Master! I give thanks to the Most High for all He has done for me and for us. I give Him all the praises and the glory! I am still a child in His eyes and still learning to walk in this thing called life. I am steadily growing in His Grace at His Mercy. I will keep praying and giving Him all the praise for saving me and protecting me in my walk of life. I lean not to my own understanding but rely totally on His! Prayer works!

He Blesses Me Still,

He Blesses Me Still.

Sandra K. Bridges

Look to the Hills

Look high to the sky,
To see with your eyes,
The mighty hand of our dream maker,
We see the trilogy of the sun,
Moon,
Stars in the skies.
Wind and the clouds write upon
The sky,
All that the master wants us to see.
The eagles underline the message
He sends,
Giving us instructions to follow thee.
Oh, how lucky are we,
To have a Father such as thee,
To care and protect us,
From hurt and harm from the
Enemy.
How marvelous to witness such
Beauty.
He has painted the fish that live in
The waters.
I see the numerous colors,
Of the wings of the butterflies.
Look how beautiful the animals are adorned.
All in various shades and hues.

I Wish You Would!

Oh, how wonderful is the hands of our Lord.
He has painted and designed every living thing.
The sounds of us all are so amazing to hear.
The song I hear is an original that only we can sing,
So we must practice, make it perfect for our heavenly guest.
For now we must find that elusive gown we will wear.
Oh, please do not forget the stars for your crown,
For it is mandatory that we wear it with our gown.
Sing Hosanna, sing Hosanna to the Highest.
I cannot wait to sing my part; I will sing from deep in my heart, way up there standing beside my Lord.
I can only imagine how wondrous it will be,
As I dream of His Majesty

Sandra K. Bridges

A Mother's Prayer

A Mother's Prayer for her children is: they are kept in the arms of the Lord Jesus, they are happy, safe, and healthy, they learn respect and responsibility, and they stay in church. She desires and prays daily that they stay away from the wrong crowds, and are not easily influenced by the outside world. She wants her children to know true love and find that special someone to walk the path of life with them.

A Mother's Prayer is far different from a Father's Prayer. A father wants his son to be what he is not and might never be. But, a mother is more concerned for the safety and protection of her children. A Mother's Prayer is said in the middle of the night when her household is asleep. She is up praying and pleading with God to keep her children under His wing

A Mother's Prayer for her girl child is that she learns self-love, self-worth, self-respect, self-confidence, independence, and determination. She wants her daughter to learn from her errors and to prosper in the male-driven world. To never accept the word no from a teacher or recruiter and never be a follower. She must learn to stand up for herself and her rights. She must not sit back and accept what someone says as fact.

A daughter must learn to always be prepared for anything and anyone. She must dress for success and know how to speak with anyone on any level. To never be afraid to speak her mind and give a good, logical, fact-filled opinion on any subject with anyone at any time. A woman must fight for her rights in a world full of old men. Don't depend on anyone and any man for your happiness; this you must already have inside you. She has taught her daughter how to pray and seek God for strength, comfort, guidance, and healing.

A Mother's Prayer for her sons and daughters is that they get a good education, that they have mastered life skills and learned to be independent. They are happy with their career goals and accomplishments. That they love, respect, and cherish her. A mother will and has sacrificed her entire life for her child's well-being and security. A mother will allow her child to stumble and fall because she realizes that they have to learn from their errors. She will always be there for them, but she cannot save them from themselves.

A mother will always encourage her children to put God first! A mother will encourage and read God's Word to her children. A mother will cry at the drop of a hat at her child's graduation, promotions, weddings, and the birth of her grandchildren. A mother will never stand in the way of her child's happiness. A mother will chastise her children no matter what age they are! She will continue to offer words of advice and guidance to her children because they are her children. A mother will always bring her children to the Lord in prayer. Some mothers have had to be both mother and father to their children. She understands she has to allow her man child to learn from a man. She will seek help at her church and school for just the right man to help her guide her man child.

A mother will do everything she can to help guide her children with love and respect. A mother will humble herself in order to nourish her spirit-person to keep up the fight for the rights of her children. A mother will guide her children, using herself as a role model. She has taught her children about self-sacrifice and determination. A mother must and has taught her children how to save for a rainy day.

A real mother has taught her children how to love by loving and respecting herself and her God through prayer and devotion. A mother's love knows no bounds when it comes to her children! It's a fight that you will never, ever win! A Mother's Prayer is, "Lord, take care and watch over my children."

Climbing Your Mountain

As a woman, I've had to learn how to climb many mountains. Jealousy from other girls in school and the workplace, boys who didn't understand why I wouldn't go out with them.

They didn't understand that I was "different" from the others. I didn't dress or speak like them. My momma prayed for me and my siblings! She said, "Daughter, you're different from them. Follow God's will! Never seek to be like someone else. You are unique, and you are stronger than you think!"

I climbed those mountains with my mother's words in my heart and a prayer on my lips. As a mother, I had to climb a mountain called Divorce, Abuse, and Single Parenting! Yes, I shed a lot of tears while climbing those mountains.

But I remembered my momma's words: "Follow God's will!" Momma was a strong, determined, and prayerful woman of God! Her prayer life as well as her faith in God inspires me daily. So, I climbed those mountains and stood on top of them!

I looked down at the valley and started shouting and praising Jesus! I've finally got the victory!

I'm an overcomer in Jesus' name!

I am an overcomer.

Sandra K. Bridges

He Blessed Me Still

Despite all my stumbles and falls, He blessed me still.
He picks me up and dusts me off
and sends me on my way again and again.
Yet, I fail to say I love you.
Despite my failings and my indiscretions,
He blesses me still.
In spite of my broken promises and unspoken prayers,
He loves me still.
He is the last person we call in our time of stress.
Yet He is the first person to come when we
are in need.
His services are free, indeed,
but still, we fail to appreciate Him and all his deeds.
Although He cries and weeps from our deceit,
He blesses us still.
Now I come again to the foot of the cross to beg,
Plead, and cry out for mercy and grace.
My Heavenly Father, we need you.
Your children need protection from their storms and rains.
Please, won't you bless us still?
I ask for forgiveness in not honoring you
when all You do is carry me and walk beside me.
You have fed, clothed, and bathed me in your love.
You have provided and sent out Your angels to
watch over me in my time of sorrow and strife.

I Wish You Would!

Despite my ungratefulness and unwillingness
to change, I pray You love me still.
Father, forgive Your humble servant.
I come to the altar to ask forgiveness in my blind and
weakened state.
Forgive my ungratefulness.
Lord, I cry out for mercy and beg for grace.
Lord, redeem me in Your blood.
Lord, You are my King of Kings, my Alpha and Omega, Lord.
I plead to You to come and bless me still.
I now understand, oh Lord, and know for certain
I cannot and will not live without Your forgiveness.
I beseech thee to give me Your love.
I demand that You hold me in the warmth of Your bosom.
You are the holder of my past, present, and future.
You must bless me still. You must bless me still.
Bless me still. Bless me still.

Sandra K. Bridges

I Praise His Holy Name

How wondrous is His name, for He is marvelous to behold. His presence is always with me. He's climbed many mountains, walked numerous roads, highways, and byways for my soul. I praise His only name. The angels sing songs of His glory. How sweet is the sound when they sing of His majesty. How sweet is the sound when the choir of birds and insects sing praises to Him! Oh, how the fields of the valley stand up and shout of His beauty, and the animals dance of His Omnipotence! I praise His only name.

The sun, moon, and the stars are impatient for their chance to shine and twinkle to announce His goodness and mercy to the universe! Oh, how marvelous is my Lord and Savior. Oh, how great is He to me, His child, to show me of His love and devotion. Praise His only name. I call Him by many names, but they all mean the same. He is my Savior and Father. He so loves this child. He is merciful and faithful to me. He is forgiving and full of grace. He is always understanding and patient with me.

I praise His only name. He never tires nor slumbers. He is always on time and never misses my appointments! His touch is soothing to my soul. He speaks softly and gently whispers His love to me. He shows his love for me in so many, many ways.

I praise His only name. He is my all in all in the midnight hour. He is my shelter in storms and rocks me to sleep. He holds me while I am suffering and weak. He wipes away all of my tears and fears. He is my comforter, protector, and healer. I praise His only name! He is my Heavenly Father, my Alpha and Omega, my beginning and my end, my sunshine and my moonlight, my clouds and my stars, my guiding light and my lightning rod, my redeemer and my soul salvation! Hallelujah!

I Praise His Holy Name.

I Praise His Holy Name!

Sandra K. Bridges

Prayer Changes Things

"For whosoever shall call upon the name of the Lord shall be saved."
(Romans 10:13 KJV)

The wind was high, the sea boisterous.
In fact, it was a real storm on Galilee.
The disciples saw what they thought was a phantom walking on the water, but their fears were calmed
by the familiar voice of Jesus. "It is I; be not afraid."
Then Peter said, "Lord, if it be thou, bid me come unto thee on the water."
Jesus said, "Come."
Peter began to walk toward Him on the water; but when he saw the raging billows, fear entered his heart, and he began to sink.
Then he prayed the shortest prayer on record.
"Lord, save me."
Jesus reached forth His hand and took him
(Matthew 14:26-31).
This is an illustration of calling on the Lord, crying out to Him as a child might cry to his mother or father in a time of danger or fear.
Jesus came to seek and save the lost.
He was born of the blessed virgin that he might "save His people from their sins" (Matthew 1:21 KJV).

That's why His name is Jesus, the Savior.
Only those who call upon the name of the Lord, only those who cry out for help, will find His salvation and are helped.
True enough, we are saved by grace through faith, and not of ourselves.
"It is the gift of God" (Ephesians 2:8 KJV).
But in another sense, we are saved by prayer.
"Whosoever shall call .... shall be saved."
This is one prayer that will always be answered in the affirmative.
The sincere cry to God for salvation will be heard.
The promise distinctly says, "Whosoever."
But no one will call upon God for salvation until they realize that they are lost.
Friends, if you need help, pray, and pray now.
Prayer changes things for you and me.

Sandra K. Bridges

Reflection:

I Wish You Would!

Section 5: She Said That

I Wish You Would

I wish you would try and tell me who I am, what I could or should be.

I ain't you and don't wanna be!

I wish you would try and hinder me. I got plans to make and you ain't nowhere in them. I got places to go. No, you ain't comin with me.

Yo, get your hands off me, man, please. You tried to keep me down. You tried to tell me I ain't nothin. You tried to mess me up—told all that negative stuff to me. You told me nobody wanted me, cause I'm too fat, cause I'm too Black, cause my hair ain't that, said my tats ain't where it's at, man. Please.

You must be talkin that mess bout yo own self. Cause that man round the way, well, he said I'm all that. He said my tats was where it's at. And my hair, well, he knows how to pull it just right. This big butt you don't like, well, he does it just right. He said you just don't know how to do this big butt of mine! Child, please.

Man, please stop talkin all that wackety wack; that smackety smack ain't where it's at. Drop that fist, man, cause ima go Madea on ya. You won't beat me again! Imma beat you like the dog you is!

I wish you would!

Ima leave you here on yo dirty flo, cryin. Ima leave you on the flo, bleeding from the beating I gave you. How did you like gettin beaten like you used to beat me?

How does it feel being treated like a dog? How does it feel to be told you ain't nothin? How does my cast iron feel? Child, please! My man is outside, waitin on me. You see he wants to take me places. He keeps his promises, and he treats me like I wanna be treated—with respect. Stop cryin like a girl. Ain't that what you used to say to me?

Man, stop begging me to stay. I thought I was nothin. Why are you begging this fat, Black nappy-haired dog? Just shut the hell up! You hear that? My man is comin. I took too long beating yo behind. I wish he would give me more time to finish your behind.

But ima lady now. Ima let you live.

I just want you to know.

Pay back, she looks just like me.

I Wish You Would!

The Devil in Disguise

He looked good and smelled better,
Dressed like a model and walked with power.
Colgate smile, spoke like a scholar.
Had lines like a pro, wooing all the ladies with his flow.
He was looking for a special lady,
One that he could use and abuse.
That special lady
Who never knew her worth.
She didn't know she was the prize.
He kept her confused and unsure.
Placed doubts in her mind.
Tied to the house in fear.
She wonders why she felt this way.
She never was this way before.
She fell to her knees in prayer.

Crying out, "Help me, Father, for I am lost!"
He said, "Where have you been?
You walked away from me! Hid yourself in fear."
My God, my God, forgive me!
Please, help me, Father!
"My child, get that man out of your house."
My man! Yes! That devil in disguise.
"You are unequally yoked to a demon.
He is hurting you and deceiving you. Get the negativity
out of your life! You must pray and look within!"
You must pray for strength and courage.
Confront him now with what I said!
You choose who you will serve on this day!
Me, or your devil in disguise!"

Is It You or Is It Me?

Is it you or is it me?
I am confused by what you are telling me.
You say you are my lover, yet you betray me.
I am puzzled by your words and actions
And how you are getting defensive by my reaction.
Now you are hurt by my anger and behavior.
Don't you think I deserve to be
Angry by your betrayal?
Is it you or is it me?
You are the one who lied to me
About our relationship, what it meant to you and me.
So how many secrets will you share today?

What will be revealed on this day?
What is really your name?
Are you really who you claim to be?
Is it you or is it me?
Had a need to lie about loving me.
How many babies do you really have?
How many baby mammas have you made?
I thought you could not have babies.
It is you who deceived me,
So don't be surprised by my actions.
You see, I found all your deceptions,
I called all your conceptions,
Contacted their representation,
Then I got my representation,
To present you with a presentation.
It is me you see. Did you forget the gun I keep?
It's always with me. Did you really forget who I be?
Must I remind you what I said?
"Do not mess with me and mine,
Cause if I find out your deceit, I will hurt and have you beat."
Yes, it's you and not me!
I do not tolerate lies and excuses.
I have been honest, truthful, and faithful.
Don't be angry that I kept my word.
I told you not to lie, cheat, or steal from me.
Did you forget I'm from the bayou?
It's a good hiding place for people like you.
I kept my word, and you will remember who I be,
A chick who you should never lie to. Yes, it is me!

I Want That Ride and Die Type of Love!

Is finding true love worth the headaches and heartaches? Is it worth my time and energy? Is having a "meaningful" relationship worth my time? Some say love makes the world go round; I say it makes the people of the world act like fools! Some people have been killed, imprisoned, and maimed in the name of love. Some say the way a woman loves a man is different than a man's love for his woman! Why is there a difference? What is this thing called love?

My definition is: love is mental, physical, emotional, spiritual, and all encompassing! It's being accepted for who and what you are! It's pleasing and satisfying to both me and you. It's about putting another person before you. It's about praying for that person more than you pray for yourself. Love is selfless and selfish at the same time! Love is God the Father, Son, and the Holy Spirit! Love is the most beautiful feeling and experience that God could ever give to us humans!

Love is a smile from a special someone, love is a touch of a lover's hand on the small of your back, love is a sweet, soft kiss, love is a physical release that only that special someone can give you, love is being served breakfast in bed by your lover after an all night love fest, love is taking care of you while you are sick, cleaning up after you, doing your shopping because you are working late, love is having dinner prepared because you got caught in traffic and delayed coming home, love is leaving love notes in your purse or briefcase, love is surprising you with flowers just because, love is a hug and your lover telling you, "Don't worry, I will take care of it for you." All of these small little things tell me of someone loving me just because I am me! He can call me in the middle of the night, and he can make love to me over the phone and can back it up when he gets home! My lover makes sure that I am sexually fulfilled all day and night by giving me multiple orgasms! My lover can give me a look and a smile that tells me he can't wait to get me home! He does not leave me wondering…about anything!

I want that ride and die type of love!

Some of that thuggish, all-night lovin!

If there is a man on this earth who can treat me like Jesus does, please send him my way! He must be an ALL-night, ride and die type of man! He must NOT be attached to another woman, not married and/or living with another woman who he is sleeping with! Show me the papers; I want proof! He must be financially stable, brings home double what I bring home, have his own car, home, no baby momma drama, and most of all, he must be heterosexual and show me his medical records! These are non-negotiable terms! He must be able to defend my honor and give body massages daily! I do reciprocate all the above terms and agreements. My lover can wear a suit during the day and rock Timberlands at night! He is educated and streetwise. My lover is nobody's fool and has the body to back it up! My love is not trying to find himself because he already has his stuff together! He is comfortable and secure with who he is and where he is going in life! My lover is not a wimp nor has the need to be reminded constantly that I am his woman and I got his back! He knows it and has confidence in his woman! This is what I am seeking at this time in my life!

I want that ride and die type of love! Some of that thuggish, all-night lovin!

If all above terms and agreements are met with my satisfaction, I do believe respect and love can grow in this environment. Because if I cannot respect you, trust you, depend upon your word in deed and action, how can I grow in love with you? I refuse to give my mind and body to someone I do not like and, most of all, do not trust! What is this thing called love? It's him loving my smell, smile, the way I walk and I talk; he gets along and shows respect to my family and friends. He understands my uniqueness and my way of thinking. This man respects me and allows me to be me! My lover does not want me to change into someone else! He does not want me to lose weight if I don't want to lose weight! After all, he fell in love with the big-boned Amazon warrior woman and not a bony stick chick! He can be my prayer partner, my soul contender, my friend in the middle of the night, my comforter after a hard day at work, and most of all, he can be my life partner! If you find this man, please send him my way! You have permission to give this man my phone number and email address!

I want that ride and die type of love! Some of that thuggish all-night lovin!

Sandra K. Bridges

Go If You Want to Go!

Go if you want to go.
Why you keep talking about it?
Why do you keep threatening to do it?
Please, just go ahead and go!
Am I supposed to beg you to stay?
You want us kids to beg you to stay.
We don't see you enough to know you.
Next time you call my momma a name,
You might not leave here the same way you came!
So, go if you want to go.
I strongly advise you to do so!
We are doing just fine without you.
Mom's been doing just fine for a long time.
We can't miss what we never had.
How can we miss someone who was never there?
Our schools don't know you,
Our bank don't know you,
And the mailman don't know you!
Please, do us all a favor and don't come back.
You are not the man that my momma first met.
The man who made all those sweet promises to her.
The man who asked her to have his babies.
The man who promised to provide for his family.
Now this same man is hurting his beloved wife and child!
At your once was and never will be!

I Wish You Would!

So, go if you want to go.
We can't miss what we never had,
A man to call husband and dad!
From your babies and the new man of the house.
Their lawyer.

Sandra K. Bridges

Fed Up

I have an announcement from on high!
But I want to make a statement before telling you what it is.
I have had enough of all your mess!
I cannot and will not take any more of your disrespect.
Now, enough is enough, and it's way too much!
Who do you think you are? Did you give birth to me?
Do I look like your child, and did I give you permission to
push me around and disrespect me anytime you please?
Do you have some type of mental problem that we should
know about? Because if you do, I will excuse your
unprofessional behavior. If you do not have a
mental dysfunction, I need to remind you of all the
EEOC rules and regulations before I go
off on you! You need to back up off of me!
I don't give a damn who you are or what title you hold.
I said back the hell up off of me!
I am tired of all your foolishness!
You whine and shuffle your feet day in and day out.
I am tired of doing your work and making excuses
for you being so useless! You make me ill every time
I think about all of you.
I am tired of you taking me for granted.
I am tired of you coming in late and then taking the credit for
my work.
When asked to explain my charts and graphs, you tell me to

I Wish You Would!

explain it to everyone.
I am fed up with your lies and undercover tricks!
Gentlemen, meet your new company manager!
Yes, the person who you lied about and degraded!
The person you told to do your presentations.
The person who did all the accounting.
Designed all the graphs and charts. The person who spoke and met with all the company officials and assistants when you were out to lunch at three in the afternoon.
Yes, it's me! When a woman is fed up, she becomes
unpredictable
and your biggest problem!

Sandra K. Bridges

Don't Try Me

Try to judge me
Try to push me
Try to discourage me
You treat me bad
Try to hate on me
Try to date on me
Try to fake me
You didn't make me
Try to shake me
Try to bite me
Try to bait me
Try to deceive me
You lost the game
I'm walking away
The winner
You tried me!

Hold This Tongue Of Mine Lord! Hold It for Me!

Well, I have been holding this tongue of mine since yesterday! Lord, it's getting harder to hold on to the reins of this stubborn tongue. It wants to bite one of them old bitties. One of them will jump straight out of her chair and flythrough the window if I say, "Boo," to her! She's one of them people who says something and then go hides in her office...scary, weak-a$$ heifer! You gotta go and get help to get your dirty work done!

Please, my Lord and Savior, hold this tongue of mine!

Hold me back, dear Jesus, from slapping some color in her face! She really does need some color in her fat, floppy cheeks. It might do her some good.

Lord, I told them to go 'head and leave me alone. Let me do my work! They do not realize who they talkin' bout! Don't they know I'm from the 504? Straight out the Hollygrove? They betta ask somebody.

Lord, I just need you to please, hold this tongue of mine! You know I hate gossip and its partner in crime called "I Do Believe" or "I assume"! They get on my last bit of nerve that I have left in me! My God! My God! What the hell do you believe, and why do you assume to know my job or anything about me? What the hell, and why? Our Father, which art in heaven?!

Hold this tongue of mine! Please, send patience down my way. Right now, Lord Jesus, right now! Racism is in full affect, and please do not believe it does not exist. Don't buy that stock, cause you will lose all ya money. Jesus said we must die daily!

Every day and all through the day, I am asking Him, "God! Hold this tongue of mine! Please, I beg You to give me patience! Rain Your strength down on me right now!"

I am always shouting and screaming for my Father to "Give me the strength to stay away from this woman. Bless me with understanding and kindness, enough to make me forgive her ignorance and not hold it against her. I must accept where she is in her life!

But, Lord Jesus, it's hard to hold this tongue of mine! I gotta read Your word daily just to make it through each day...why, Lord?

I love my job, I really do. So, I'll continue to beg and plead for You to hold this tongue of mine! Thanks be to You, that I left my daddy's switchblade at home in my jewelry box! Cause I sho coulda released some of that fluid around them fat ankles...Lord Jesus, I gotta stay on bended knee!

Reflection:

Sandra K. Bridges

About the Author

Sandra Bridges was born and raised in the soulful city of New Orleans, Louisiana. From an early age, she knew the power of perseverance and faith. She attended Oakwood College in Huntsville, Alabama, where she majored in psychology and management. In her freshman year, she was offered a co-op position in civilian personnel, opening the door to a career in federal service—her first step into a world that would test, mold, and uplift her.

She returned to Louisiana and continued her federal employment while raising her children with love, strength, and a whole lot of crockpot cooking. With her kids' blessing and teamwork in the kitchen, Sandra re-enrolled in school. Her son learned to cook with spices, and her daughter mastered the George Foreman grill. She graduated from Southern University at New Orleans in 2001, a proud moment for a mother whose children were forging their own paths: her daughter at Howard University and her son training at Parris Island with the United States Marine Corps.

When Hurricane Katrina struck, Sandra relocated to Washington, DC. It was during this season that God inspired her passion for poetry, prayer, and motivation. She found herself not only doing her job but living her purpose! Her memories of praying with survivors of abuse, encouraging women in shelters, and sowing seeds of faith through her own testimony flowed through her poetry & writing. She reminded them, and herself, that with God's Word and Grace, healing was possible.

God later led Sandra to a workplace of peace and purpose. Though leaving was difficult, it marked the end of nearly eighteen years in federal service—a journey full of growth, challenges, and blessings. Today, Sandra continues to write, speak, and inspire. You can find her speaking on Divine Destiny Prayer Line. Their information is on Facebook. She also recommends her church prayer Line: Monday–Friday @ 8a.m., United Fellowship SDA on Facebook and YouTube. With both these lines, she stays centered and spirit-filled!

As a published author, Sandra uses her gifts to uplift women from all walks of life, especially those who've walked through fire and come out refined!

You can find Ms. Bridges on:

Facebook, Instagram, and Messenger @Skbridges4real

On LinkedIn: Skay4real

Her ebook is available at: https://payhip.com/b/KzjBY

For speaking engagements or appearances, please contact her through any of the platforms above.

www.ingramcontent.com/pod-product-compliance
Lightning Source LLC
Chambersburg PA
CBHW070848160426
43192CB00012B/2358